WELCOME TO THE 2018 MANCHESTER UNITED ANNUAL!

For fans all over the world, of all ages, this is the perfect celebration of the Reds.

For starters, you can get to know all about the first team squad. Every single senior player is profiled in detail, with loads of little-known facts about Jose Mourinho's lads.

One of them – Juan Mata – sits down with the Annual to chat about his massive social media presence and his charity work, while we also look at the great aid provided by United's Foundation since it was formed a decade ago.

On the subject of history, you can marvel at United's record as the most successful club in English football and look at all of the trophies we've won, including the three we scooped during the 2016/17 season.

There's all this and plenty more besides in the 2018 Manchester United Annual, including a series of Reds-related brain-teasers to test your club knowledge, plus the chance to win a home shirt signed by first team squad members!

Enjoy, and remember to keep the Red flag flying high…

PLAYER PROFILES

GET TO KNOW MOURINHO'S MEN: THE 2017/18 MANCHESTER UNITED FIRST TEAM SQUAD...

2017/18 SQUAD LIST

1. DAVID DE GEA
2. VICTOR LINDELOF
3. ERIC BAILLY
4. PHIL JONES
5. MARCOS ROJO
6. PAUL POGBA
8. JUAN MATA
9. ROMELU LUKAKU
10. ZLATAN IBRAHIMOVIC
11. ANTHONY MARTIAL
12. CHRIS SMALLING
14. JESSE LINGARD
15. ANDREAS PEREIRA
16. MICHAEL CARRICK

17. DALEY BLIND
18. ASHLEY YOUNG
19. MARCUS RASHFORD
20. SERGIO ROMERO
21. ANDER HERRERA
22. HENRIKH MKHITARYAN
23. LUKE SHAW
25. ANTONIO VALENCIA
27. MAROUANE FELLAINI
31. NEMANJA MATIC
36. MATTEO DARMIAN
38. AXEL TUANZEBE
40. JOEL PEREIRA
45. KIERAN O'HARA

1
DAVID
DE GEA

POSITION: GOALKEEPER
BORN: 7 NOVEMBER 1990; MADRID, SPAIN
PREVIOUS CLUB: ATLETICO MADRID
JOINED UNITED: 29 JUNE 2011

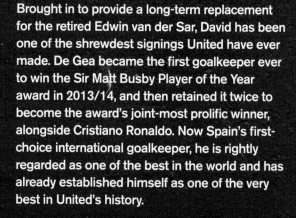

DID YOU KNOW?

WHEREAS HIP-HOP AND GRIME REGULARLY PLAY IN THE OLD TRAFFORD DRESSING ROOM, DAVID IS A HUGE HEAVY METAL FAN. IN EARLY 2017, HE WENT BACKSTAGE AT THE MANCHESTER ARENA TO MEET AMERICAN BAND AVENGED SEVENFOLD, HIS FAVOURITE GROUP.

BEST BITS

LIGHTNING REACTIONS, QUICK THINKING AND THE SAFEST HANDS IN THE BUSINESS.

Brought in to provide a long-term replacement for the retired Edwin van der Sar, David has been one of the shrewdest signings United have ever made. De Gea became the first goalkeeper ever to win the Sir Matt Busby Player of the Year award in 2013/14, and then retained it twice to become the award's joint-most prolific winner, alongside Cristiano Ronaldo. Now Spain's first-choice international goalkeeper, he is rightly regarded as one of the best in the world and has already established himself as one of the very best in United's history.

2

VICTOR LINDELOF

POSITION: DEFENDER
BORN: 17 JULY 1994, VASTERAS, SWEDEN
PREVIOUS CLUBS: VASTERAS, BENFICA
JOINED UNITED: 1 JULY 2017

BEST BITS

AS WELL AS HIS IMPOSING PHYSIQUE, VICTOR IS ALSO EXCELLENT AT BRINGING THE BALL OUT FROM THE BACK.

DID YOU KNOW?

LINDELOF IS SUCH A COOL, CHILLED-OUT CHARACTER THAT HIS TEAM-MATES AT BENFICA, HIS FORMER CLUB, GAVE HIM THE NICKNAME 'THE ICEMAN'.

The Swedish international defender became Jose Mourinho's first summer signing ahead of the 2017/18 campaign, and his transfer from Benfica was a move designed to bring extra class to United's defence. Victor made his breakthrough into senior football at the age of 16 in Sweden before moving to Portugal, where he gradually played his way into Benfica's first team and became one of the best young defenders in Europe. A three-time Portuguese league winner with Champions League experience, Lindelof is strong, fast and also a very calm influence at the back, whether at right-back or in his preferred position in central defence.

3

ERIC
BAILLY

POSITION: DEFENDER
BORN: 12 APRIL 1994, BINGERVILLE, IVORY COAST
PREVIOUS CLUBS: ESPANYOL, VILLARREAL
JOINED UNITED: JUNE 2016

BEST BITS

POWER AND POSITIVITY MAKE
BAILLY A DOMINANT DEFENDER.

DID YOU KNOW?

ERIC IS FRIENDS WITH FORMER CHELSEA
STRIKER DIDIER DROGBA, WHO IS SUCH A
HERO IN THEIR NATIVE IVORY COAST THAT HE
ONCE MANAGED TO END A CIVIL WAR IN
THE COUNTRY.

After just two full seasons of senior
football in Spain's La Liga, Eric Bailly
was something of an unknown quantity
when he became Jose Mourinho's
first-ever signing as Manchester United
manager. By the end of the defender's
first season at Old Trafford, however,
he was a key part of the Reds' central
defence and tipped to remain there
for years to come. The Ivory Coast
international is an incredible athlete,
blessed with pace, strength and bravery.
While he is more than capable with the
ball at his feet, he also knows when to
be no-nonsense, and plenty of opposing
strikers already have tales of the
Ivorian's tough-tackling!

4

PHIL
JONES

POSITION: DEFENDER
BORN: 21 FEBRUARY 1992; PRESTON, ENGLAND
PREVIOUS CLUB: BLACKBURN ROVERS
JOINED UNITED: 1 JULY 2011

BEST BITS

THE ENGLAND INTERNATIONAL IS AN EXPERT READER OF THE GAME, ALLOWING HIM TO PREVENT DANGEROUS SITUATIONS DEVELOPING.

An England international who puts his body on the line for the cause, Phil Jones is a wholehearted defender. He first came to Sir Alex Ferguson's attention while playing against United for Blackburn Rovers, his first club, and he was bought ahead of the 2011/12 season. He has lifted the Premier League, FA Cup, League Cup and Europa League during his time at Old Trafford, and is now one of the longest-serving players at the club. Though he has featured at right-back and in defensive midfield occasionally, his primary position has always been a central defender, and no striker is in for an easy 90 minutes against Jones.

DID YOU KNOW?

A BOYHOOD BLACKBURN FAN, PHIL'S FAVOURITE-EVER CHRISTMAS PRESENT WAS A ROVERS SHIRT FEATURING THE NAME OF PERUVIAN STRIKER ROQUE SANTA CRUZ!

5

MARCOS
ROJO

POSITION: DEFENDER
BORN: 20 MARCH 1990; LA PLATA, ARGENTINA
PREVIOUS CLUBS: ESTUDIANTES, SPARTAK
MOSCOW, SPORTING LISBON
JOINED UNITED: 20 AUGUST 2014

Though injury has hampered his United story to date, Marcos Rojo has shown some of the best football of his career during his time at Old Trafford. Signed in 2014 after starring in Argentina's run to the World Cup final, Marcos quickly showed that he could play in a variety of defensive positions for the Reds. His best season to date was the 2016/17 campaign, when he excelled under Jose Mourinho, and he was a major reason behind United's fine defensive record. His season was cruelly cut short by a cruciate knee ligament injury in April 2017, but he tackled his recovery like everything else: by giving it everything he's got.

DID YOU KNOW?

MARCOS'S BOYHOOD HERO WAS EX-UNITED PLAYMAKER JUAN SEBASTIAN VERON, WHO HE LATER PLAYED WITH AT ESTUDIANTES.

BEST BITS

A MASTER OF THE DARK ARTS OF DEFENDING, INCLUDING SOME HEFTY CHALLENGES.

PAUL
POGBA

POSITION: MIDFIELDER
BORN: 15 MARCH 1993;
LAGNY-SUR-MAME, FRANCE
PREVIOUS CLUBS: LE HAVRE, JUVENTUS
JOINED UNITED: 8 AUGUST 2016

BEST BITS

SHOWMANSHIP, SKILL, ATHLETICISM.
AND THE LIST GOES ON.

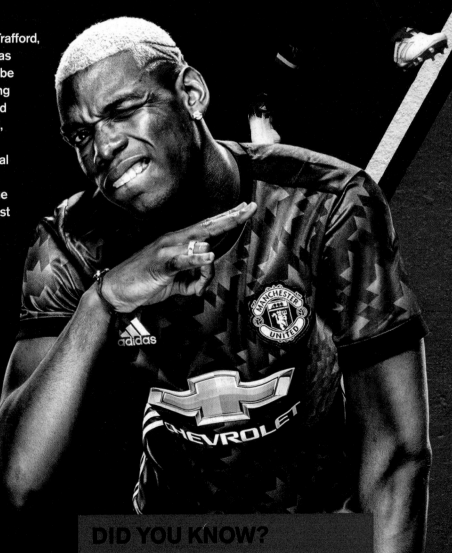

During his first spell at Old Trafford, everybody inside the club was sure that Paul Pogba would be a superstar. After his stunning development at Juventus and subsequent return to United, they have all been proven right. The French international midfielder is now one of the most influential players in the team and one of the very best in the world. Pogba loves to show everybody what he can do with the ball, and there are very few things he can't do! He has a huge range of passing, great pace and power, plus a knack for scoring big goals at important times – such as the Europa League final. Better still, he does it all with a smile on his face, making him a huge figure in the dressing room.

DID YOU KNOW?

IN JANUARY 2017, PAUL BECAME THE FIRST
FOOTBALLER TO HAVE HIS OWN EMOJI ON TWITTER!

8

JUAN
MATA

POSITION: MIDFIELDER/FORWARD
BORN: 28 APRIL 1988, BURGOS, SPAIN
PREVIOUS CLUBS: VALENCIA, CHELSEA
JOINED UNITED: 25 JANUARY 2014

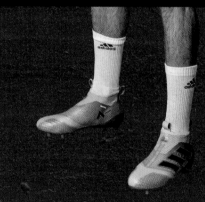

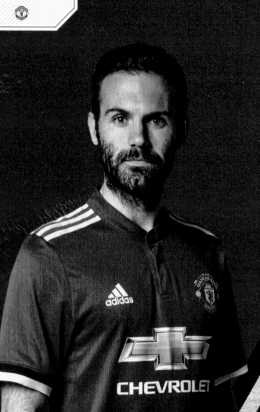

BEST BITS

THE SILKIEST FIRST TOUCH YOU'LL SEE,
AND A BRAIN AS SHARP AS THEY COME.

DID YOU KNOW?

JUAN IS A KEEN TRAVELLER, AND DURING
THE SUMMER HE REGULARLY DONS HIS
BACKPACK AND GOES OFF IN SEARCH OF
ADVENTURE AROUND THE WORLD.

Renowned as one of the nice guys of football, Juan Mata is more than just the smiley Spaniard who stars on social media and regularly helps out children's charities. The former Valencia and Chelsea playmaker is one of the Premier League's most skilful forwards, boasting movement and vision which few defenders can cope with. Whether he plays behind a lone striker or either side of a front three, Mata's brilliant left foot gives him the ability to unlock the tightest of defences, and his importance is underlined by the fact that, since his arrival, he has been picked to start all three of United's cup finals.

9
ROMELU
LUKAKU

POSITION: FORWARD
BORN: 13 MAY 1993, ANTWERP, BELGIUM
PREVIOUS CLUBS: ANDERLECHT, CHELSEA,
WEST BROMWICH ALBION (LOAN), EVERTON
JOINED UNITED: 10 JULY 2017

BEST BITS

THERE AREN'T ANY STRONGER PLAYERS
IN THE PREMIER LEAGUE. HE'S ALSO
FAST AND A DEADLY FINISHER.

When Jose Mourinho was looking for a target
man to bring power and presence, it didn't
take him long to settle on Romelu Lukaku.
The giant Belgian had spent the last four
seasons tearing up the Premier League with
Everton, and his array of skills made the
move something of a no-brainer, even if it
did take a colossal fee to bring him to Old
Trafford. Romelu has a huge amount of
experience for such a young striker, having
been first called up to Belgium's senior
international squad when he was just 16,
and his arrival makes United extremely
intimidating in attack.

DID YOU KNOW?

ROMELU IS CLOSE FRIENDS WITH PAUL POGBA, AND
WAS ON HOLIDAY WITH THE FRENCHMAN IN LOS
ANGELES WHEN HE DECIDED TO SIGN FOR UNITED!

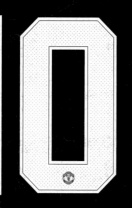

10

ZLATAN
IBRAHIMOVIC

POSITION: STRIKER
BORN: 3 OCTOBER 1981; MALMO, SWEDEN
PREVIOUS CLUBS: MALMO, AJAX, JUVENTUS,
INTERNAZIONALE, BARCELONA, AC MILAN,
PARIS ST GERMAIN
JOINED UNITED: 24 AUGUST 2017

You've heard of this guy, right? Zlatan Ibrahimovic arrived at Old Trafford in the summer of 2016 with a history of winning with every club he'd represented, and sure enough, he played a huge role in winning three more trophies during his first season in Manchester. Far and away United's top scorer in 2016/17 with 28 goals, the giant Swede suffered a serious knee ligament injury near the end of the season. After his contract expired, however, he regained fitness and re-signed with the Reds to take care of unfinished business at Old Trafford.

BEST BITS

HE'S BIG, HARD AND BRILLIANT, BUT PERHAPS MOST IMPORTANTLY HE DRIVES STANDARDS AND PROVIDES THE WINNING MENTALITY NEEDED IN A SUCCESSFUL DRESSING ROOM.

DID YOU KNOW?

ZLATAN HAS WON 33 TROPHIES DURING HIS CAREER. FOR PERSPECTIVE, THAT MEANS HE'S WON MORE TROPHIES THAN ALMOST EVERY CLUB IN ENGLISH FOOTBALL – THE ONLY EXCEPTIONS BEING UNITED, LIVERPOOL AND ARSENAL!

11

ANTHONY
MARTIAL

POSITION: FORWARD
BORN: 5 DECEMBER 1995; MASSY, FRANCE
PREVIOUS CLUBS: LYON, MONACO
JOINED UNITED: 1 SEPTEMBER 2015

Few United fans had heard of Anthony Martial before he joined the Reds in 2015, but a stunning solo goal on his debut against Liverpool quickly made him a household name. Over the coming weeks and months, he repeatedly demonstrated an incredible knack for scoring goals whenever the chance arose. He shone as a centre forward in his first season at Old Trafford, before moving into a wider role in his second term. From the wing, Martial's incredible speed with and without the ball, plus his dazzlingly quick feet, makes him a nightmare for any defender to contend with, and he is a vital part of United's attacking ranks.

BEST BITS

PACE, CLOSE CONTROL AND A CALM HEAD IN FRONT OF GOAL.

DID YOU KNOW?

ANTHONY HAS FOLLOWED SOME FAMOUS FOOTSTEPS, PLAYING FOR CLUB OMNISPORTS DES ULIS, THE SAME YOUTH TEAM AS FORMER FRANCE STARS PATRICE EVRA AND THIERRY HENRY.

12

CHRIS
SMALLING

POSITION: DEFENDER
BORN: 22 NOVEMBER 1989;
GREENWICH, ENGLAND
PREVIOUS CLUBS: MAIDSTONE UNITED, FULHAM
JOINED UNITED: 7 JULY 2010

BEST BITS

AT HIS MOST PROACTIVE AND DOMINANT, FEW ATTACKERS CAN GET THE BETTER OF SMALLING, WHOSE STRENGTH AND PACE ARE A FORMIDABLE COMBINATION.

One of only seven current squad members to have played for United in the Sir Alex Ferguson era, Chris Smalling is one of the most experienced defenders on the Reds' books. In his seven seasons at Old Trafford, he has developed from a promising youngster into a regular captain of the first team, learning from the likes of Rio Ferdinand and Nemanja Vidic along the way. A full England international, Chris has won the Premier League, FA Cup, League Cup and Europa League during a glorious few years – an incredible rise for a player who was playing non-league football two years before joining the Reds.

DID YOU KNOW?

BEFORE HE JOINED FULHAM IN 2008, CHRIS WAS PLANNING TO STUDY FINANCIAL ECONOMICS AT UNIVERSITY.

14

JESSE
LINGARD

POSITION: FORWARD
BORN: 15 DECEMBER 1992;
WARRINGTON, ENGLAND
PREVIOUS CLUBS: NONE
JOINED UNITED: 1 JULY 2009

DID YOU KNOW?

KNOWN FOR HIS INTRICATE GOAL
CELEBRATIONS, JESSE OFTEN PRACTICES
NEW DANCES SO THAT THEY'RE READY
FOR THE NEXT TIME HE SCORES.

One of the great modern success stories of
United's Academy system, Jesse has been
with the Reds since the age of seven. A late
developer physically, he had to play with
lower age groups while he rose through
the Reds' ranks, and also needed several
loan spells to get first team experience.
Even a serious knee injury on his
long-awaited United debut couldn't
dampen his ambition, however, and
Jesse eventually played his way into
first team regularity in 2015/16, after
which he went on to score in the
finals of the FA Cup and League
Cup, and he is a huge, happy part
of Jose Mourinho's squad.

BEST BITS

UPERB MOVEMENT, TACTICAL
SIGHT PLUS A KNACK FOR
CORING GOALS WHICH ARE
OTH SPECTACULAR AND VITAL.

15

ANDREAS
PEREIRA

POSITION: MIDFIELDER/FORWARD
BORN: 1 JANUARY 1996; DUFFEL, BELGIUM
PREVIOUS CLUBS: PSV EINDHOVEN
JOINED UNITED: 1 JULY 2012

BEST BITS

TECHNICAL ABILITY AND FABULOUS DELIVERY
OF THE BALL – ESPECIALLY FREE-KICKS.

While relegation might not have been an ideal end to his loan spell at La Liga's Granada, Andreas Pereira took huge strides in his development during the 2016/17 term. The Brazilian youth international was the star of the Spanish side's season, playing virtually every week and putting in a series of outstanding displays, sparking hope that he can make it as a first team regular at United. Opportunities have been few and far between for Andreas, largely because of the quality of other players in his preferred position as a support striker, but his ability to also play a deeper midfield role should open the door for more chances.

DID YOU KNOW?

ANDREAS CITES CRISTIANO RONALDO AS HIS BIGGEST IDOL, AND
WAS ABLE TO TEST HIMSELF AGAINST THE EX-UNITED WINGER
WHEN GRANADA FACED REAL MADRID DURING HIS LOAN SPELL.

16

MICHAEL
CARRICK

POSITION: MIDFIELDER
BORN: 29 JULY 1981, WALLSEND
PREVIOUS CLUBS: WEST HAM,
TOTTENHAM HOTSPUR
JOINED UNITED: 31 JULY 2006

When Wayne Rooney left Old Trafford in the summer of 2017, Jose Mourinho quickly identified Michael Carrick as the right man to become his captain. The veteran midfielder not only has an unrivalled amount of experience of life at the club, he also remains one of the coolest, calmest midfielders around. Carrick is a brilliant shield for United's defence, while also providing the starting point of many attacks, thanks to his intelligence and foresight. He has evolved into one of the classiest English midfielders of modern times, and his presence at Old Trafford sets the standard for professionalism and football intellect.

BEST BITS

EXPERIENCE, VISION AND A SUBLIME RANGE OF PASSING. HE'S ALWAYS ONE STEP AHEAD!

DID YOU KNOW?

AFTER BEING GRANTED A TESTIMONIAL IN 2017, THE SKIPPER SET UP THE MICHAEL CARRICK FOUNDATION WHICH GIVES OPPORTUNITIES TO YOUNG PEOPLE IN MANCHESTER AND NEWCASTLE.

17

DALEY
BLIND

POSITION: DEFENDER/MIDFIELDER
BORN: 9 MARCH 1990; AMSTERDAM, NETHERLANDS
PREVIOUS CLUB: AJAX
JOINED UNITED: 1 SEPTEMBER 2014

In his first three seasons as a Red, Dutch international Daley Blind performed admirably in various roles on the field. Having emerged in Ajax's first team as a left-back, he also demonstrated his ability in defensive midfield, starring in both positions as his boyhood club won four successive Dutch league titles. Since moving to United, he has also played as a left wing-back, but more often on the left side of central defence. Wherever he plays, Daley brings his enormous football brain to the role. He can outwit most opponents and ensures he is always one step ahead, bringing high-level thinking to United's team.

BEST BITS

HUGE INTELLIGENCE AND INSIGHTFUL READING OF THE GAME.

DID YOU KNOW?

ONE OF THE BIGGEST INFLUENCES ON DALEY'S LIFE WAS FRANK DE BOER, HIS BOSS AT AJAX, WHO JOINED HIM IN ENGLAND IN 2017 WHEN HE TOOK THE MANAGER'S ROLE AT CRYSTAL PALACE.

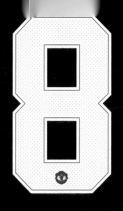

18

ASHLEY
YOUNG

POSITION: DEFENDER/WINGER
BORN: 9 JULY 1985; STEVENAGE, ENGLAND
PREVIOUS CLUBS: WATFORD, ASTON VILLA
JOINED UNITED: 1 JULY 2011

ong-serving Red who has evolved his game
amatically since moving to United from
ton Villa. When he arrived at Old Trafford,
hley Young was already deemed
rsatile enough to play on either wing or
hind a lone striker, but recent years
ve seen him also add defensive
es to his list of abilities. It was Louis
n Gaal who first used Young as a
ng-back, then a full-back, and his
aptability has prompted Jose
urinho to continue to find a
riety of roles for the man he
ers to as "our joker, who
n play in any position."
ring his time with the
ds, Ash has won six
phies, including four
ferent major honours.

BEST BITS

VERSATILITY, TACTICAL DISCIPLINE AND
A DEADLY COLLECTION OF CROSSING.

DID YOU KNOW?

AS A CHILD, YOUNG WAS IN THE
SAME SCHOOL YEAR AS FORMULA
ONE STAR LEWIS HAMILTON.

19

MARCUS
RASHFORD

POSITION: FORWARD
BORN: 31 OCTOBER 1997;
MANCHESTER, ENGLAND
PREVIOUS CLUBS: NONE
JOINED UNITED: 1 JULY 2014

One of the sensations of recent times in English football, Marcus only got his first team chance because of an injury to Anthony Martial in February 2016. The Mancunian teenager stepped up and promptly scored twice on his debut, then bagged two more in his second game, and was a first-team star from then on. He quickly received a call-up to the England national team and – guess what – scored again on his debut. After undergoing a huge growth spurt during 2016/17, picking up more experience and bagging some key goals, it's little surprise that Marcus is rated as one of the great young hopes for club and country. An absolutely enormous talent and a brilliant professional.

BEST BITS

PACE, FEARLESSNESS AND A HUGE VARIETY OF FINISHING.

DID YOU KNOW?

MARCUS WAS SPOTTED BY UNITED WHILE PLAYING FOR FLETCHER MOSS, THE SAME LOCAL YOUTH TEAM WHICH JESSE LINGARD PLAYED FOR.

20

SERGIO
ROMERO

POSITION: GOALKEEPER
BORN: 22 FEBRUARY 1987;
BERNARDO DE IRIGOYEN, ARGENTINA
PREVIOUS CLUBS: RACING CLUB,
AZ ALKMAAR, SAMPDORIA, MONACO (LOAN)
JOINED UNITED: 27 JULY 2015

BEST BITS

A COMPLETELY POSITIVE MINDSET, GREAT
CONCENTRATION AND SUPERB SHOT-STOPPING.

Widely regarded as the best
back-up goalkeeper around,
Sergio Romero has provided
the perfect cover for David De
Gea, impressing Jose Mourinho
enough to star in the Reds'
successful Europa League
campaign of 2016/17. The
Argentina international has
remained first choice for his
country, despite not starting
regularly at club level, and his
form whenever selected for
United has been spotless. He
kept an amazing 12 clean sheets
in 19 appearances in 2016/17,
including one against Ajax in
the Europa League final, and
extended his contract with the
Reds in the summer of 2017.

DID YOU KNOW?

EVEN THOUGH THEY ARE COMPETING
FOR ONE SPOT IN THE TEAM, SERGIO
AND DAVID DE GEA ARE FIRM FRIENDS
– JOSE MOURINHO HAS ADMITTED
THAT HE HAS NEVER KNOWN TWO
GOALKEEPERS TO BE SO CLOSE!

21 ANDER HERRERA

POSITION: MIDFIELDER
BORN: 14 AUGUST 1989; BILBAO, SPAIN
PREVIOUS CLUBS: REAL ZARAGOZA, ATHLETIC CLUB
JOINED UNITED: 26 JUNE 2014

BEST BITS

TIRELESS WORKRATE AND INTELLIGENCE MAKE HIM A NON-STOP HUB OF MIDFIELD ACTIVITY.

DID YOU KNOW?

ANDER ONLY HAS ONE PRE-MATCH RITUAL: HE ALWAYS TRIES TO TEXT HIS MUM BEFORE EACH MATCH.

An all-action midfielder who quickly became a fans' favourite when he arrived at Old Trafford in 2014, Ander Herrera enjoyed his best season so far for United in 2016/17. Now a full Spanish international, Ander thrived under Jose Mourinho, bringing tonnes of energy and clever play to the Reds' midfield, where he operates either in a shielding role in front of the defence, or a more advanced role in support of a lone striker. Herrera first came to United's attention when he starred for Athletic Club when they knocked the Reds out of the Europa League in the 2011/12 season, and his arrival in 2014 marked the end of a long chase!

22

HENRIKH
MKHITARYAN

POSITION: FORWARD
BORN: 21 JANUARY 1989; YEREVAN, ARMENIA
PREVIOUS CLUBS: PYUNIK, METALURH DONETSK,
SHAKHTAR DONETSK, BORUSSIA DORTMUND
JOINED UNITED: 6 JULY 2016

BEST BITS

PACE, VISION, BRAINS: HENRIKH HAS EVERYTHING
AN ELITE MODERN FORWARD NEEDS.

It took a few months for Henrikh Mkhitaryan to adapt to English football, but once he did, he showed himself to be one of most exciting, effective players on United's books. He is fast enough to be a sprinter – a career he admits he would have pursued, had he not made it in football – but is also devastating with the ball. He ended his first season with the clinching second goal in the Europa League final win over Ajax, a strike which was later voted United's goal of the month for May – an award he also won in four of the previous five months!

DID YOU KNOW?

MKHITARYAN IS A KEEN SUPPORTER
OF CHARITIES AND REGULARLY
SPENDS TIME PROMOTING WORTHY
CAUSES. HE IS A GOODWILL
AMBASSADOR FOR PROMINENT
CHILDREN'S CHARITY UNICEF.

23

LUKE
SHAW

POSITION: DEFENDER
BORN: 12 JULY 1995; KINGSTON-UPON-THAMES, ENGLAND
PREVIOUS CLUB: SOUTHAMPTON
JOINED UNITED: 27 JUNE 2014

BEST BITS

DEVASTATING PACE, SKILL ON THE BALL AND A TERRIFIC ENGINE. HE'S ALSO A DEEPLY POPULAR FIGURE AT THE AON TRAINING COMPLEX.

It says a lot for Luke Shaw's ability that he is still widely regarded as the Reds' outstanding left-back despite not yet realising his full potential at Old Trafford. His first season after joining from Southampton was a steady campaign, but a brilliant start to his second term was ended by a broken leg and injury also ravaged 2016/17 for the luckless defender. Luke retains the faith of Jose Mourinho, however, and the Portuguese recognises that the England international brings a combination of attributes a modern full-back needs: namely an ability to contribute huge amounts to the team at both ends of the pitch.

DID YOU KNOW?

LUKE RECKONS HE IS THE FASTEST PLAYER AT THE CLUB, JUST AHEAD OF MARCUS RASHFORD.

25

ANTONIO
VALENCIA

POSITION: DEFENDER
BORN: 4 AUGUST 1986; LAGO AGRIO, ECUADOR
PREVIOUS CLUBS: EL NACIONAL,
VILLARREAL, WIGAN
JOINED UNITED: 30 JUNE 2009

Only Michael Carrick has been in United's first team longer than Antonio Valencia, who arrived at Old Trafford in 2009 after the departure of Cristiano Ronaldo. For the first half of his Reds career, Antonio was a highly effective winger, and won the Reds' 2011/12 Player of the Year award as an attacker. After undergoing a positional change, however, he has gradually become an outstanding right-back – one of the best in the world – and as a defender he was voted 2016/17 Player of the Year by his team-mates. His importance to the United cause has been underlined by showers of praise from all around the club, and he had the huge honour of starting the Europa League final as United's captain.

DID YOU KNOW?

ANTONIO'S HOMETOWN, NUEVA LOJA IN ECUADOR, IS IN THE AMAZON RAINFOREST!

BEST BITS

INCREDIBLE STAMINA, SPEED, STRENGTH AND HEART.

27

MAROUANE FELLAINI

POSITION: MIDFIELDER/FORWARD
BORN: 22 NOVEMBER 1987; ETTERBEEK, BELGIUM
PREVIOUS CLUBS: STANDARD LIEGE, EVERTON
JOINED UNITED: 2 SEPTEMBER 2013

Whether a deep-lying midfielder or further up the field as a support striker or even an emergency centre forward, Marouane Fellaini adds a different dimension to United's play whenever he is on the field. Signed from Everton after a series of impressive displays against the Reds, the giant Belgian international quickly set about making himself known at Old Trafford. In his four full seasons with the Reds, he has popped up with crucial contributions in huge games, not least in 2016's successful FA Cup run, and his contribution to the United cause is there for all to see.

BEST BITS

STAMINA, PHYSICAL TOUGHNESS AND THE ABILITY TO PROVIDE THE REDS WITH AN ALTERNATIVE APPROACH WHENEVER THE SITUATION DEMANDS IT.

DID YOU KNOW?

OF ALL THE PLAYERS HE HAS FACED IN HIS CAREER, MAROUANE NAMES FORMER REDS CAPTAIN NEMANJA VIDIC AS HIS TOUGHEST OPPONENT.

31

NEMANJA MATIC

POSITION: MIDFIELDER
BORN: 1 AUGUST 1988, SABAC, SERBIA
PREVIOUS CLUBS: FK KOLUBARA, KOSICE, CHELSEA, BENFICA, CHELSEA
JOINED UNITED: 31 JULY 2017

One of the most important signings of the Jose Mourinho era, Nemanja Matic is a player who the United manager knows better than most – after all, he's already bought him once before! The Serbian international left Chelsea for Benfica in 2011, but was quickly brought back to Stamford Bridge by Jose in 2014. The result? Two Premier League titles in three years for the enormous midfielder, who reads the game better than most and always knows the right place to be at the right time. A massive signing in more ways than one.

BEST BITS

A POWERFUL, INTELLIGENT PRESENCE IN MIDFIELD, NEMANJA IS AN EXPERT WHEN IT COMES TO PROTECTING UNITED'S DEFENCE AND STARTING ATTACKS.

DID YOU KNOW?

ONE OF MATIC'S HEROES IS HIS NAMESAKE, FORMER UNITED CAPTAIN NEMANJA VIDIC. THE PAIR WERE INTERNATIONAL TEAM-MATES FOR SERBIA AND REMAIN FRIENDS TO THIS DAY.

36

MATTEO
DARMIAN

POSITION: DEFENDER
BORN: 2 DECEMBER 1989; LEGNANO, ITALY
PREVIOUS CLUBS: AC MILAN, PADOVA (LOAN),
PALERMO, TORINO
JOINED UNITED: 11 JULY 2015

BEST BITS

VERSATILITY, POSITIONAL DISCIPLINE
AND TERRIFIC CONCENTRATION.

DID YOU KNOW?

AS A PRODUCT OF AC MILAN'S
YOUTH ACADEMY, MATTEO IDOLISED
CLUB LEGEND PAOLO MALDINI,
AND MANAGED TO GET THE ITALY
LEGEND'S MATCH-WORN SHIRT
BEFORE HE RETIRED.

Italian defenders are renowned as some
of the most disciplined in world football,
and Matteo Darmian has continued that
trend since arriving at Old Trafford ahead
of the 2015/16 season. Initially used as
a right-back, he has subsequently shown
the ability to operate just as capably on
the left side of defence, ensuring plenty of
first-team outings for the consistent Italian.
His move to England has been hugely
successful, with winners' medals in the FA
Cup, League Cup and Europa League after
just two seasons, and Matteo's impressive
nous gives him an important defensive role
to play in the Reds' ongoing evolution.

38

AXEL
TUANZEBE

POSITION: DEFENDER/MIDFIELDER
BORN: 14 NOVEMBER 1997, BUMIA, DEMOCRATIC
REPUBLIC OF CONGO
PREVIOUS CLUBS: NONE
JOINED UNITED: 1 JULY 2013

BEST BITS

LEADERSHIP AND A COOL
TEMPERAMENT ALLOW AXEL TO HOLD
HIS OWN IN SENIOR FOOTBALL.

One of the stars of the club's
Academy, Axel Tuanzebe is rated
very highly by the club's coaching
staff. Not only can he perform in
central defence or at right-back,
but under Jose Mourinho he has
also demonstrated the capability
to reach Premier League level
in midfield. Axel has previously
voiced an ambition to be United's
future captain, and his early
senior displays for the Reds have
demonstrated that he has the
ability to be whatever he puts his
mind to. Not only is he excellent
with and without the ball, he also
has an astonishing maturity for one
so young.

DID YOU KNOW?

THOUGH HE WAS BORN IN THE
DEMOCRATIC REPUBLIC OF CONGO,
AXEL WAS RAISED IN ROCHDALE AND
REPRESENTS ENGLAND AT YOUTH LEVEL.

40

JOEL PEREIRA

POSITION: GOALKEEPER
BORN: 28 JUNE 1996;
BOUDEVILLIERS, SWITZERLAND
PREVIOUS CLUB: NEUCHATEL XAMAX
JOINED UNITED: 1 JULY 2012

BEST BITS

THIS GUY IS ABSOLUTELY MASSIVE,
BUT SUPER AGILE WITH IT.

Jose Mourinho has already tipped
Joel Pereira to be Portugal's
best goalkeeper in the coming
years, and the hype around this
brilliant young stopper continues
to build. Like most 'keepers, Joel
is physically imposing and he
fills the goal with his giant frame.
Since joining the Reds in 2012, he
steadily rose through the youth
ranks before impressing during
a loan move to Rochdale, and he
was promoted to the first team
squad in 2015/16. Jose rates the
youngster very highly and his first
two senior outings during the
2016/17 campaign resulted in
clean sheets; a trend which can
gladly continue!

DID YOU KNOW?

FOR YEARS, PEOPLE HAVE MADE THE MISTAKE
OF THINKING THAT JOEL AND ANDREAS PEREIRA
ARE BROTHERS, BUT THEY JUST HAVE THE SAME
SURNAME. "HE'S MY BROTHER FROM ANOTHER
MOTHER," SAYS ANDREAS.

45

KIERAN
O'HARA

POSITION: GOALKEEPER
BORN: 22 APRIL 1996; MANCHESTER, ENGLAND
PREVIOUS CLUBS: NONE
JOINED UNITED: 1 JULY 2012

After first coming to United's attention at just eight years old, Kieran O'Hara has grown into one of the best young goalkeepers at the club. The Manchester-born shot-stopper has already been on five loan deals during his short career to date, including an important work-experience placement loan at non-league Trafford, where he learnt his trade and grew up quickly. Since then, after being promoted to the first team squad at United, he has trained with the Reds' senior goalkeepers at the Aon Training Complex and was rewarded with a senior squad number to wear during the 2017/18 campaign.

BEST BITS

GREAT REFLEXES AND A WEALTH OF LOAN EXPERIENCE FOR SUCH A YOUNG GOALKEEPER.

DID YOU KNOW?

THOUGH HE WAS BORN IN MANCHESTER AND HAS REPRESENTED ENGLAND SCHOOLS, KIERAN HAS CHOSEN TO REPRESENT THE REPUBLIC OF IRELAND AT INTERNATIONAL LEVEL. HE IS ELIGIBLE BECAUSE HE HAS IRISH GRANDPARENTS.

AND THE REDS

GO MARCHING ON ON ON!

2016/17 REVIEWED

JOSE MOURINHO'S FIRST YEAR AS
UNITED MANAGER ENDED WITH THE
REDS LIFTING THREE TROPHIES – NOT
BAD, EH?! HERE'S A LOOK BACK AT HOW
WE GOT ON LAST SEASON

COMMUNITY SHIELD:
STARTING WITH SILVERWARE

Having won the FA Cup in 2015/16, United went up against reigning Premier League champions Leicester City at Wembley in the 2016/17 season opener. Jesse Lingard's superb solo goal set the Reds underway, and though Jamie Vardy equalised for the Foxes, debutant Zlatan Ibrahimovic headed in a late winner to do what he always does: bag silverware!

REDS SAID

"I'VE BEEN HERE A COUPLE OF WEEKS AND I GET TO WIN MY FIRST TROPHY WITH UNITED. THIS IS WHAT WE PLAY FOR."
ZLATAN IBRAHIMOVIC

PREMIER LEAGUE:
DRAWS DENT HOPES

REDS SAID

"GENERALLY, THE PERFORMANCES WERE VERY GOOD AT HOME. WE JUST COULDN'T FIND A WAY TO BREAK TEAMS DOWN. I'M SURE WE'LL GET THERE. WE'LL IMPROVE."
MICHAEL CARRICK

During the 2016/17 campaign, United set a new club record for successive unbeaten league matches, going 25 straight games without defeat between October and May. However, too many drawn games during that run prevented the Reds from seriously contesting the title race and, in the end, Mourinho's men had to settle for a sixth-place finish. There was some cause for optimism, however. United lost just five league games all season – as many as champions Chelsea – and had the second-best defence in the division, conceding just 29 goals in 38 games. What's more, the best performance of the season came when Jose masterminded a dominant 2-0 win over his former club Chelsea, who didn't even manage a single shot on target all game at Old Trafford. With better finishing, particularly at home, it could have been a different story for United.

EFL CUP:
ZLATAN TIME!

United lifted the League Cup for the fifth time in the club's history after a tricky campaign lined with Premier League opponents. The Reds opened with a routine 3-1 win at Northampton Town, but after that each opponent came from England's top division, including Manchester City, who were beaten by Juan Mata's fine finish at Old Trafford. West Ham were swatted aside in the quarter-final, before a 3-2 aggregate win over Hull City in the semi-finals. That led to a meeting with Southampton at Wembley in the final, and United were strolling to victory after taking an early two-goal lead through Ibrahimovic and Lingard. A quick double from Manolo Gabbiadini drew Southampton level though, and the Reds had to hold on before snatching a late victory when Zlatan brilliantly headed in Ander Herrera's cross. Before the end of February, the first two trophies of the season had both gone to Old Trafford!

REDS SAID

"MANCHESTER UNITED HAS GOT A HISTORY OF WINNING TROPHIES. WE'VE GOT A KNACK FOR WINNING AND AS SOON AS YOU GET THAT WINNING FEELING, YOU ALWAYS WANT MORE."

JESSE LINGARD

FA CUP:
A CONTROVERSIAL EXIT

REDS SAID

"THE GAME WAS COMPLETELY UNDER CONTROL. I THINK EVERYONE SAW THE MATCH UNTIL THE RED CARD. AFTER THAT, I WANT TO SAY THAT I'M REALLY PROUD OF MY PLAYERS."

JOSE MOURINHO

The Reds' early rounds in the FA Cup went as smoothly as possible, with Reading and Wigan Athletic both thumped 4-0 at Old Trafford before Blackburn Rovers were beaten 2-1 at Ewood Park, with Zlatan once again getting a late winner. The quarter-final draw was unkind, pitting the Reds with a tricky away tie at Premier League leaders Chelsea, but Jose's tactics completely stopped the Blues from dominating the game until the harsh decision to give Herrera a red card midway through the first half. United ended up losing the game 1-0, but could take a lot of pride from competing so well with only 10 men.

40

EUROPA LEAGUE:

United had won every available trophy before, with one exception: the Europa League. To change that fact, the Reds would need to play a mammoth 15 games, the last of which was the final in Stockholm.

The campaign began with a tricky group stage which provided home and away meetings with Feyenoord, Zorya Luhansk and Fenerbahce. Though United lost both opening away games, three straight home wins and a final win at Zorya booked a spot in the knockout stages. Saint Etienne were eased out, 4-0 on aggregate, with Ibrahimovic hitting a hat-trick at Old Trafford and Henrikh Mkhitaryan scoring the only goal of the away leg.

Our midfield Armenian then scored in a 1-1 draw at Russia's FC Rostov, before Juan Mata finished the job back in Manchester with the only goal of the second leg. Micki was at it again in the quarter-final, scoring home and away against Anderlecht, but it took an extra-time winner from Marcus Rashford to secure a place in the semi-finals.

United's gifted young local striker scored a brilliant free-kick against Spain's Celta Vigo in the away leg, before a nervous return at Old Trafford finished 1-1 and the Reds booked a trip to Stockholm for the final.

Ajax were our opponents in Sweden, and another tactical masterclass from Jose completely shut down the dangerous Dutch side. Paul Pogba's first-half opener put the Reds ahead, before Micki turned in yet another goal to make the game safe and give United not only the final missing trophy, but also a return to the Champions League!

REDS SAID

"WE WANTED TO WIN THIS TROPHY AS WELL FOR THE CITY OF MANCHESTER AND WE HAVE BROUGHT THE TROPHY BACK. IT'S MASSIVE FOR US AND I'M SO HAPPY!"

JUAN MATA

ALL THE TROPHIES

NO CLUB IN ENGLISH FOOTBALL HAS WON MORE TROPHIES THAN UNITED, AND THE 2016/17 EUROPA LEAGUE SUCCESS FILLED IN THE ONLY REMAINING GAP IN THE OLD TRAFFORD TROPHY CABINET. OUR HUGE HAUL OF 66 HONOURS STACKS UP LIKE THIS...

**PREMIER LEAGUE/
FIRST DIVISION**

20

**FA
CUP**

12

**LEAGUE
CUP**

5

**COMMUNITY/CHARITY
SHIELD**

21

**UEFA CHAMPIONS
LEAGUE/EUROPEAN CUP**

3

**UEFA EUROPA
LEAGUE**

1

**UEFA CUP
WINNERS' CUP**

1

**UEFA
SUPER CUP**

1

**INTERCONTINENTAL
CUP**

1

**FIFA CLUB
WORLD CUP**

1

TOP OF THE PILE
MOST HONOURS WON IN ENGLISH FOOTBALL...

1. **UNITED – 66**
2. LIVERPOOL – 61
3. ARSENAL – 46
4. CHELSEA – 29
5. TOTTENHAM – 25

LAST SEASON'S EUROPA LEAGUE AND EFL CUP DOUBLE WAS THE EIGHTH TIME UNITED HAVE WON MORE THAN TWO MAJOR HONOURS IN THE SAME SEASON...

1991/92

UEFA SUPER CUP, LEAGUE CUP

1993/94

PREMIER LEAGUE, FA CUP

1995/96

PREMIER LEAGUE, FA CUP

1998/98

PREMIER LEAGUE, FA CUP, UEFA CHAMPIONS LEAGUE

1999/2000

INTERCONTINENTAL CUP, PREMIER LEAGUE

2007/08

PREMIER LEAGUE, UEFA CHAMPIONS LEAGUE

2008/09

FIFA CLUB WORLD CUP, LEAGUE CUP, PREMIER LEAGUE

2016/17

LEAGUE CUP, UEFA EUROPA LEAGUE

THE ULTIMATE RED

MICHAEL CARRICK'S BRAIN
NOT ONLY THE MOST EXPERIENCE IN THE SQUAD, THE SKIPPER ALSO HAS UNRIVALLED VISION AND THE ABILITY TO DICTATE THE FLOW OF A GAME.

JOSE MOURINHO'S SQUAD HAS SOME INCREDIBLE PLAYERS WITH A WIDE RANGE OF INDIVIDUAL STRENGTHS. JUST IMAGINE WHAT WOULD HAPPEN IF YOU COULD TAKE THE BEST PARTS OF THE SQUAD AND COMBINE THEM INTO ONE EXTRA-SPECIAL SUPER PLAYER…

ROMELU LUKAKU'S FRAME
GO ON, TRY TO GET THE BALL OFF HIM. YOU CAN'T, CAN YOU?

ERIC BAILLY'S TOUGHNESS
ABSOLUTELY NO-NONSENSE WHEN HE'S IN GAME MODE, THE IVORIAN IS AS HARD AS NAILS.

ANDER HERRERA'S ENERGY
THE SPANISH MIDFIELDER IS ABSOLUTELY NON-STOP, BUZZING AROUND THE FIELD AS IF HE'S SWALLOWED AN ENGINE.

PAUL POGBA'S SKILL
FOR IMAGINATION, VISION AND TRICKERY, NONE CAN GET NEAR OUR MIDFIELD TALISMAN.

LUKE SHAW'S PACE
IN A SQUAD FULL OF FAST PLAYERS, LUKE GETS THE NOD AS THE QUICKEST. GREASED LIGHTNING.

MARCUS RASHFORD'S FINISHING
THE LOCAL LAD IS INCREASINGLY DEADLY IN FRONT OF GOAL, AND HIS WIDE RANGE OF FINISHING MAKES HIM A CONSTANT THREAT.

JUAN MATA'S LEFT FOOT
THE LITTLE MAGICIAN CAN MAKE ANYTHING HAPPEN WITH THAT WAND OF A LEFT FOOT.

CHRIS SMALLING'S HEADING ABILITY
NOBODY FANCIES AN AERIAL CHALLENGE AGAINST THE ENGLAND DEFENDER, WHO CAN BE AN UNSTOPPABLE FORCE IN THE AIR.

DAVID DE GEA'S COMMUNICATION
PART OF DAVID'S STATUS AS THE WORLD'S BEST GOALKEEPER IS HIS EXPERT COMMUNICATION WITH HIS TEAM-MATES.

MAROUANE FELLAINI'S CHEST
KICK THE BALL AS HIGH AND AS HARD AS YOU LIKE; THE BIG BELGIAN CAN CONTROL ANYTHING ON HIS CHEST.

ANTONIO VALENCIA'S POWER
THIS MAN IS A MACHINE. MAYBE LITERALLY. IS THERE A PLAYER IN THE GAME AS STRONG AS HIM? NOPE.

PHIL JONES'S GUTS
A DEFENDER WHO ONCE TACKLED AN OPPONENT WITH HIS HEAD, AT FLOOR LEVEL. BRAVERY REDEFINED.

JESSE LINGARD'S MOVEMENT
NOW YOU SEE HIM, NOW YOU DON'T. OUR LOCAL HERO CONSTANTLY KEEPS DEFENDERS GUESSING.

NEMANJA MATIC'S TACKLING
WITH THOSE HUGE, TELESCOPIC LEGS, THE SERBIAN CAN DISPOSSESS ANYBODY FROM ANYWHERE!

DALEY BLIND'S PASSING
WHEREVER HE IS ON THE PITCH, THE DUTCHMAN CAN PICK OUT HIS MAN UNERRINGLY.

ANDREAS PEREIRA'S FREE KICKS
THE YOUNG BRAZILIAN IS DEADLY FROM SET-PIECES, EITHER CROSSING OR SHOOTING.

HENRIKH MKHITARYAN'S RIGHT FOOT
OUR MIDFIELD ARMENIAN CAN DAZZLE OPPONENTS, WHETHER HE'S PASSING OR SHOOTING WITH HIS SUPER-ACCURATE RIGHT PEG.

EXCLUSIVE INTERVIEW

JUAN MATA

WITH OVER 20 MILLION FOLLOWERS SPREAD AROUND THE WORLD, JUAN MATA'S SOCIAL MEDIA ACCOUNTS ARE AMONG THE MOST POPULAR IN ENGLISH FOOTBALL. HE USES THEM TO TALK ABOUT FOOTBALL, HIS PERSONAL LIFE AND HIS IMPORTANT CHARITY WORK, AND HERE THE SKILFUL SPANIARD TELLS THE 2018 MANCHESTER UNITED ANNUAL ALL ABOUT IT...

JUAN, WHAT FIRST MADE YOU INTERESTED IN STARTING SOCIAL MEDIA ACCOUNTS?

The interaction with the fans. I have always had great respect for the fans, I myself am a football fan so I know what football means to other people, and sometimes we don't get enough interaction with them. I think it's important to make fans feel like they're a key part of the game, because they are. Without them we would be nothing. When I started doing Facebook, Twitter and Instagram it coincided with the explosion of social media, so that's why I started. I thought it was a good way of communicating with them.

AS WELL AS TALKING ABOUT FOOTBALL, YOU USE YOUR INSTAGRAM ACCOUNT TO SHOW PEOPLE PICTURES FROM YOUR TRAVELS. WHICH PLACES HAVE YOU PARTICULARLY ENJOYED VISITING?

There are so many – I like to see as many new places as I can. Recently I was in Iceland because my sister was living there and we went there as a family to visit her. It was great. You see things there that you cannot see anywhere else in the world. You can go to a massive volcano, then a waterfall, then a glacier, all on the same one big road around the country. It's a mix of great nature at its best and you cannot see the same things together anywhere else.

(Laughs) So many! I haven't been to Latin America, not as much as I would like. Argentina, Brazil, Colombia, Chile, Peru, I would like to visit them more. Australia as well.

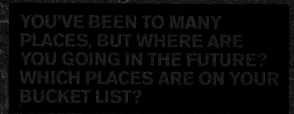

YOU HAVE PLEDGED ONE PERCENT OF YOUR WAGES TO THE FOOTBALL CHARITY COMMON GOAL, SO HOW IMPORTANT IS SOCIAL MEDIA GOING TO BE TO HELP WITH YOUR ONGOING CHARITY WORK?

Social media is one of the best ways to do it. It has a big impact around the world. Some footballers and other people help charity without publicity – and that's completely perfect and I agree with that – but in my work with Common Goal, a special project, I think it needed to be known by my fellow team-mates and professionals around the world, so that's why we did it this way. I can speak about things through interviews with newspapers, TV channels or radio stations, but social media is key to getting our message out there.

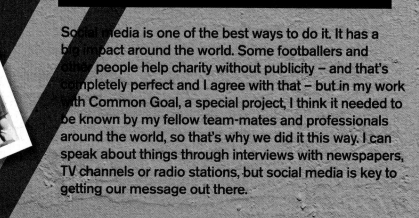

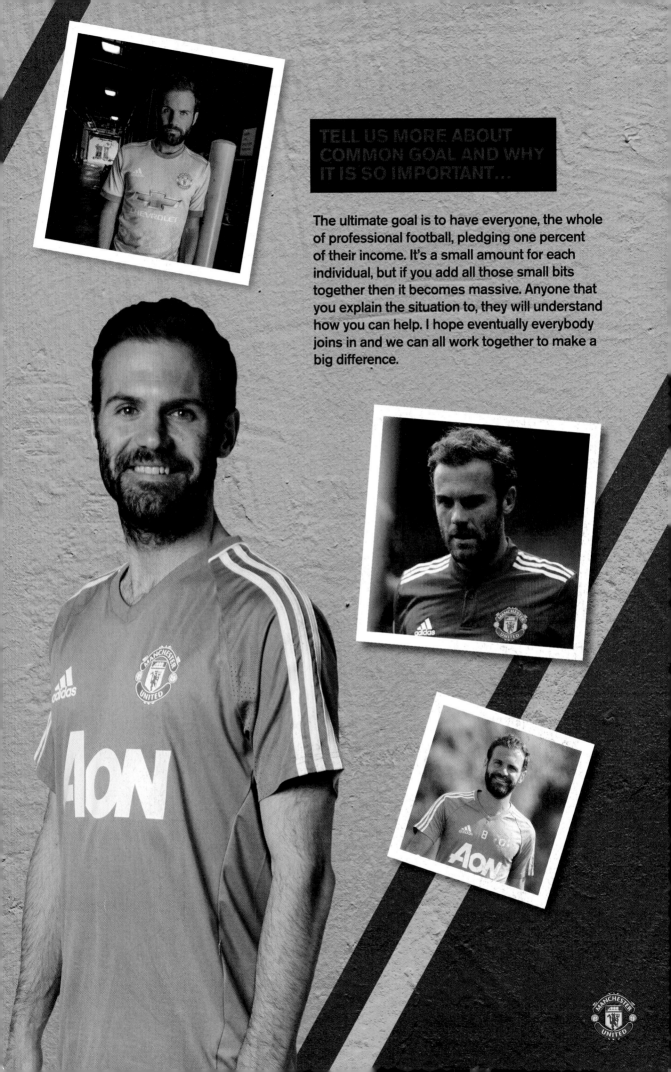

The ultimate goal is to have everyone, the whole of professional football, pledging one percent of their income. It's a small amount for each individual, but if you add all those small bits together then it becomes massive. Anyone that you explain the situation to, they will understand how you can help. I hope eventually everybody joins in and we can all work together to make a big difference.

10 YEARS OF GIVING

Foundation

THE MANCHESTER UNITED FOUNDATION HAS BEEN USING FOOTBALL TO IMPROVE THE LIVES OF YOUNG PEOPLE SINCE 2007. IN CELEBRATION OF A DECADE OF STERLING WORK, WE LOOK BACK ON THE WIDE RANGE OF EVENTS THE FOUNDATION HAS PUT ON – FROM HUGE CONCERTS AND LEGENDS MATCHES TO PERSONAL MEETINGS BETWEEN PLAYERS AND FANS…

2007

SUPPORTERS WERE TREATED TO A MEET-AND-GREET WITH THEIR UNITED HEROES, INCLUDING CRISTIANO RONALDO.

2009

OLD TRAFFORD THREW OPEN ITS DOORS AS SUPPORTERS FLOCKED TO WATCH THE FIRST TEAM IN AN OPEN TRAINING SESSION.

2010

FOOTBALL AND MUSIC COLLIDED AT UNITED RELIEF, DEMONSTRATED AS COMEDIAN PADDY MCGUINNESS GATECRASHED THE SATURDAYS' PRE-MATCH SET.

2012

PATIENTS AT ROYAL MANCHESTER CHILDREN'S HOSPITAL RECEIVED UNEXPECTED GIFTS FROM UNITED'S PLAYERS JUST BEFORE CHRISTMAS.

2013

OLD TRAFFORD PLAYED HOST TO SOME ALL-TIME GREATS IN A THRILLING LEGENDS MATCH BETWEEN FORMER PLAYERS FROM UNITED AND REAL MADRID.

2014

SIR ALEX FERGUSON VISITED THE FOUNDATION'S PARTNER SCHOOL, MANCHESTER ENTERPRISE ACADEMY, TO OFFICIALLY OPEN A SERIES OF NEW 3G PITCHES.

2015

DAVID DE GEA SHOWED OFF HIS BASKETBALL SKILLS WHEN HE VISITED BURNAGE ACADEMY FOR BOYS FOR A MULTI-SPORTS SESSION.

2016

BUDDING GOALKEEPER SAMUEL, WHO HAS CEREBRAL PALSY, WAS JOINED BY ANTHONY MARTIAL AND SAM JOHNSTONE TO TURN ON OLD TRAFFORD'S CHRISTMAS LIGHTS!

Foundation

2017

YOUNGSTERS GOT THE CHANCE TO MEET WAYNE ROONEY, THE REDS' ALL-TIME LEADING GOALSCORER, AND HIS TEAM-MATES AT THE AON TRAINING COMPLEX.

2017

IT'S ZLATAN TIME! THE BIG MAN POSED FOR SELFIES WITH FANS WHO VISITED UNITED'S TRAINING GROUND FOR ONE OF THE FOUNDATION'S DREAM DAYS.

QUIZZES AND PUZZLES

GOAL OR NO GOAL?

LOOK AT THE FOLLOWING EIGHT PHOTOS FROM 2016/17 – HALF OF THESE SHOTS RESULTED IN GOALS. CAN YOU REMEMBER WHETHER UNITED SCORED OR NOT?

A

B

C

D

E

F

G

H

1
_____ , BOSNICH, BARTHEZ, HOWARD, VAN DER SAR, DE GEA

HINT: THE GREATEST DANE OF ALL, AND ONE OF THE BEST GOALKEEPERS IN HISTORY

3
IRWIN, P NEVILLE, _____ , SHAW, BAILLY

HINT: A FRENCH INTERNATIONAL LEFT-BACK AND SOCIAL MEDIA SENSATION WHO #LOVESTHISGAME

6
PALLISTER, STAM, BLANC, BROWN, _____ , POGBA

HINT: A BOYHOOD RED FROM NORTHERN IRELAND

9
MCCLAIR, COLE, SAHA, _____ , FALCAO, MARTIAL, IBRAHIMOVIC, LUKAKU

HINT: A SLICK BULGARIAN WHO WAS UNITED'S RECORD BUY – UNTIL JUAN MATA'S ARRIVAL

15
BLACKMORE, TOMLINSON, POBORSKY, BLOMQVIST, CHADWICK, KLEBERSON, _____ , JANUZAJ, PEREIRA

HINT: A SERBIAN WARRIOR WHO BECAME UNITED'S CLUB CAPTAIN IN 2010

19
_____ , JOHNSEN, YORKE, RICARDO, DJEMBA-DJEMBA, VAN DER SAR, PIQUE, WELBECK, WILSON, RASHFORD

HINT: THIS ENGLAND INTERNATIONAL CURRENTLY HEADS THE REDS' ACADEMY

24
SCHOLES, BECKHAM, O'KANE, _____ , FLETCHER, FOSU-MENSAH

HINT: THE HARDEST MAN IN ALL THE TOWN. ORANGE HAIR. BEWARE.

27
G NEVILLE, COOKE, SILVESTRE, _____ , FELLAINI

HINT: ITALIAN STRIKER WHO SCORED ONE OF THE MOST IMPORTANT PREMIER LEAGUE GOALS IN 2009.

ANSWERS ON PAGE 60

```
R  F  E  L  L  A  I  N  I  A
A  F  E  H  A  U  C  O  I  N  N
S  C  O  A  E  I  K  C  T  O
H  A  U  L  T  R  N  A  H  L  L
F  R  E  A  E  E  R  N  K  S
O  R  M  R  L  D  I  E  F  U
R  I  E  A  R  R  N  O  R  K
D  C  V  R  U  A  I  I  T  A
E  K  L  O  A  R  I  R  L  M
N  I  M  A  M  A  T  A  N  S
```

Words go horizontally, vertically, diagonally and backwards.

LUKAKU	RASHFORD	MOURINHO	FELLAINI	HERRERA
...ARRICK	LINDELOF	MATA	VALENCIA	MATIC

NAME THE SEASON

CAN YOU MATCH THE TROPHY CELEBRATION TO THE CORRECT SEASON?

1999/2000   2002/03   2005/06   2007/08

2009/10   2012/13   2016/17

ANSWERS ON PAGE 60

SPOT THE DIFFERENCE

CAN YOU SPOT WHAT'S MISSING IN THE SECOND PICTURE COMPARED TO THE FIRST? THERE ARE EIGHT CHANGES!

FACT OR FICTION?

1. UNITED'S FIRST EVER MASCOT WAS A FOX WHICH COULD PREDICT THE FUTURE.

2. OLD TRAFFORD IS THE CLUB'S THIRD STADIUM.

3. THE CLUB'S FIRST SUPERSTAR, BILLY MEREDITH, CHEWED TOOTHPICKS DURING GAMES.

4. SIR MATT BUSBY USED TO PLAY FOR MANCHESTER CITY AND LIVERPOOL.

5. DENIS LAW ONCE SCORED 102 GOALS IN A SEASON FOR THE REDS.

6. RYAN GIGGS, PAUL SCHOLES, DAVID BECKHAM, GARY NEVILLE AND NICKY BUTT ALL PLAYED IN THE SAME YOUTH TEAM.

7. UNITED WON THE FIRST EVER PREMIER LEAGUE TITLE IN 1993/94.

8. SIR ALEX FERGUSON ALMOST RETIRED FROM MANAGEMENT IN 2002.

9. NO PLAYER PROVIDED MORE ASSISTS FOR WAYNE ROONEY AT UNITED THAN PAUL SCHOLES.

10. ROMELU LUKAKU WEARS SIZE 13.5 FOOTBALL BOOTS.

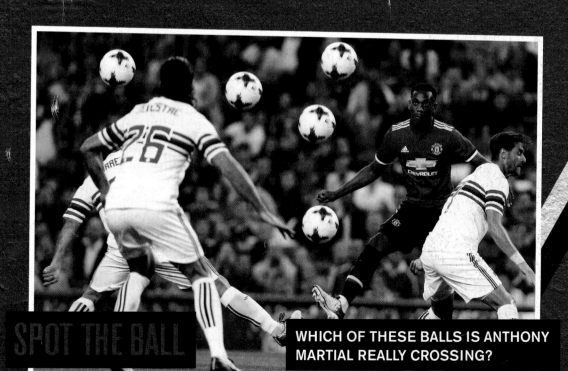

SPOT THE BALL

WHICH OF THESE BALLS IS ANTHONY MARTIAL REALLY CROSSING?

QUIZ ANSWERS

R	F	E	L	L	A	I	N	I	A
A	F	E	H	A	U	C	O	I	N
S	C	O	A	E	I	K	C	T	O
H	A	U	L	T	R	N	A	H	L
F	R	E	A	E	E	R	N	K	S
O	R	M	R	L	D	I	E	F	U
R	I	E	A	R	R	N	O	R	K
D	C	V	R	U	A	I	I	T	A
E	K	L	O	A	R	I	R	L	M
N	I	M	A	M	A	T	A	N	S

GOAL OR NO GOAL? PAGE 54

PIC A: NO GOAL
PIC B: NO GOAL
PIC C: GOAL
PIC D: NO GOAL
PIC E: GOAL
PIC F: NO GOAL
PIC G: GOAL
PIC H: GOAL

WHAT'S IN A NUMBER? PAGE 55

#1 SCHMEICHEL
#3 EVRA
#6 EVANS
#9 BERBATOV
#15 VIDIC
#19 BUTT
#24 BROWN
#27 MACHEDA

NAME THE SEASON, PAGE 57

2009/10

2012/13

2005/06

2002/03

2007/08

2016/17

1999/2000

SPOT THE DIFFERENCE, PAGE 58

FACT OR FICTION, PAGE 59

1. FICTION. IT WAS A GOOSE, THOUGH IT WENT BY THE NAME OF THE 'BANK STREET CANARY'.

2. FACT. THE REDS MOVED TO OLD TRAFFORD IN 1910, HAVING PREVIOUSLY USED NORTH ROAD AND BANK STREET.

3. FACT. BILLY ALSO PLAYED FOR THE REDS UNTIL HE WAS ALMOST 47 YEARS OLD.

4. FACT. THE LEGENDARY UNITED MANAGER WAS A DISTINGUISHED PLAYER FOR BOTH OF OUR LOCAL RIVALS.

5. FICTION. EVEN THE LAWMAN COULDN'T MUSTER THAT MANY – HIS 46 GOALS OF 1963/64 IS A CLUB RECORD.

6. FACT. THE FIVE PLAYERS ALL FEATURED FOR THE FAMOUS 'CLASS OF '92' YOUTH TEAM.

7. FICTION. IT WAS 1992/93.

8. FACT. HE WAS DUE TO RETIRE AT THE END OF THE 2001/02 SEASON, BUT CHANGED HIS MIND.

9. FICTION. AMAZINGLY, SCHOLESY ASSISTED JUST ONE OF ROONEY'S 253 GOALS.

10. FACT. JUAN MATA HAS DESCRIBED THE BELGIAN'S FOOTWEAR AS "THE BIGGEST BOOTS EVER!"

SPOT THE BALL, PAGE 59

TO BE IN WITH A CHANCE OF WINNING A 2017/18 MANCHESTER UNITED HOME SHIRT SIGNED BY FIRST TEAM SQUAD MEMBERS, YOU NEED ONLY ANSWER ONE SIMPLE QUESTION, THE ANSWER TO WHICH APPEARED EARLIER IN THE BOOK...